Counting
Butterflies
1-2-3

Brian Enslow

Enslow Elementary
an imprint of

Enslow Publishers, Inc.
40 Industrial Road
Box 398
Berkeley Heights, NJ 07922
USA

http://www.enslow.com

Enslow Elementary, an imprint of Enslow Publishers, Inc.

Enslow Elementary® is a registered trademark of Enslow Publishers, Inc.

Library of Congress Cataloging-in-Publication Data

Enslow, Brian.
  Counting butterflies 1-2-3 / Brian Enslow.
    p. cm. — (All about counting bugs 1-2-3)
  Summary: "Learn about bugs, and counting to ten"— Provided by publisher.
  Includes bibliographical references and index.
  ISBN 978-0-7660-3921-6
  1. Butterflies—Juvenile literature. 2. Counting—Juvenile literature. I. Title. II. Title:
Counting butterflies one, two, three.
  QL544.2.E57 2012
  513.2'11—dc23   2011014453

Paperback ISBN: 978-1-59845-246-4

Printed in the United States of America

052011 Lake Book Manufacturing, Inc., Melrose Park, IL

10 9 8 7 6 5 4 3 2 1

To Our Readers: We have done our best to make sure all Internet Addresses in this book
were active and appropriate when we went to press. However, the author and the publisher
have no control over and assume no liability for the material available on those Internet
sites or on other Web sites they may link to. Any comments or suggestions can be sent by
e-mail to comments@enslow.com or to the address on the back cover.

✪ Enslow Publishers, Inc., is committed to printing our books on recycled paper. The paper
in every book contains 10% to 30% post-consumer waste (PCW). The cover board on the
outside of each book contains 100% PCW. Our goal is to do our part to help young people
and the environment too!

Cover and Illustration Credits: Butterflies: Dmytruk Olena/Shutterstock.com; Cover
Background: SkillUp/Shutterstock.com; Inside Background: filip323/Shutterctock.com.

Note to Parents and Teachers

Help pre-readers get a jumpstart on reading. These simple texts introduce new concepts
with repetition of words and short simple phrases. Photos and illustrations fill the pages
with color and effectively enhance the text. Free Educator Guides are available for this
series at www.enslow.com. Search for the **All About Counting Bugs 1-2-3** series by name.

Contents

Words to Know

butterfly   one   ten

1

one butterfly

2

two butterflies

3

three butterflies

4

four butterflies

5

five butterflies

6

six butterflies

7

seven butterflies

8

eight butterflies

9

nine butterflies

10

ten butterflies

Read More

Davis, Rebecca F. *10, 9, 8 Polar Animals!: A Counting Backward Book*. Mankato, MN: Capstone Press. 2006.

Horwood, Annie. *Butterfly, Butterfly: What Colors Do You See?* New York, NY: Little Simon, 2001.

Web Sites

Cartoonito
<http://www.cartoonito.co.uk/games/how-many>
The Butterfly Site.
<http://www.thebutterflysite.com/>

Index

Guided Reading Level: **A**
Guided Reading Leveling System is based on the guidelines recommended by Fountas and Pinnell.

Word Count: **20**